DISRUPTIVE BUSINESS IDIOMS FOR VIRTUAL ENTREPRENEURS

MANIFESTOS FOR SUCCESS

DR. ELISABETH MUSIL

COPYRIGHT & PERMISSIONS

INTRODUCTION

Creativity and opportunity for virtual entrepreneurs is at a cusp.
As a professor, coach, and consultant, I am continually inspired by dynamic entrepreneurs who want to disrupt industries and forge new paths towards success. Higher order thinking is required to infuse voguish enterprises to innovate within a shifting global environment. In response to a call for visionary inspiration, I have compiled this work of contemporary business phraseology. It is with this intention, that the phases in this book prompt you to meditate, brainstorm, innovate, and create transformative processes.

How to use this book: select an idiom and journal on its meaning to you and your organization. Useful journaling means can include mind-mapping, writing, and creating actionable strategy. Implement your vision and watch your business evolve.

I hope this book inspires your entrepreneurial creativity and success.

Dr. Elisabeth Musil

lizmusilconsultants.com
drlizmusil.com

Rancho Palos Verdes, CA

DR. ELISABETH MUSIL

APPROPRIATELY SCALE

EXCEPTIONAL IDEAS

DYNAMICALLY SEIZE STAND-ALONE RESULTS

DR. ELISABETH MUSIL

PHOSFLUORESCENTLY PURSUE SUPERIOR METHODS OF EMPOWERMENT

SEAMLESSLY RE-ENGINEER CUTTING-EDGE CLOUDS

DR. ELISABETH MUSIL

APPROPRIATELY PRODUCTIZE

EMPOWERED LEADERSHIP

EFFICIENTLY INNOVATE EQUITY INVESTED IMPERATIVES

COLLABORATIVELY STREAMLINE END-TO-END SOLUTIONS

PROACTIVELY ACTUALIZE 24/365 INFRASTRUCTURES

DR. ELISABETH MUSIL

PHOSFLUORESCENTLY IMPACT ROBUST ACTION ITEMS

CONTINUALLY LEVERAGE EXISTING PERFORMANCE BASED ROI

DR. ELISABETH MUSIL

CONVENIENTLY CONCEPTUALIZE AN EXPANDED ARRAY OF E-BUSINESS

INTRINSICALLY MAXIMIZE MAGNETIC MARKETS

DR. ELISABETH MUSIL

COMPELLINGLY SYNDICATE REVOLUTIONARY WEB-READINESS

PROFESSIONALLY RE-ENGINEER PROFESSIONAL PROCESS IMPROVEMENTS

PROFESSIONALLY EXPEDITE

LEADING-EDGE

METHODOLOGIES

GLOBALLY SYNTHESIZE REVOLUTIONARY PARADIGMS

HOLISTICALLY DELIVER HIGH-QUALITY WEB-READINESS

OBJECTIVELY SCALE DISTRIBUTED IDEAS

DYNAMICALLY PROVIDE ACCESS TO PROGRESSIVE SYNERGY

UNIQUELY WHITEBOARD RESOURCE-MAXIMIZING SERVICES

DR. ELISABETH MUSIL

ENTHUSIASTICALLY REDEFINE COMPELLING ALIGNMENTS

PROACTIVELY INCUBATE OPTIMAL NICHE MARKETS

DR. ELISABETH MUSIL

ENTHUSIASTICALLY EVOLVE CLIENT-CENTRIC E-MARKETS

HOLISTICALLY INNOVATE ENTERPRISE RESOURCES

PROGRESSIVELY ORCHESTRATE
GO FORWARD PARADIGMS

PROFESSIONALLY EXTEND MULTIMEDIA BASED METHODOLOGIES

DR. ELISABETH MUSIL

COMPLETELY TRANSITION AN EXPANDED ARRAY OF INTELLECTUAL CAPITAL

ASSERTIVELY SCALE BEST-OF-BREED PROCESSES

ENERGETICALLY WHITEBOARD INTUITIVE E-COMMERCE

COLLABORATIVELY DEPLOY SUPERIOR ROI

COMPETENTLY REINVENT COST EFFECTIVE NICHES

HOLISTICALLY CLOUDIFY EMERGING FUNCTIONALITIES

DR. ELISABETH MUSIL

GLOBALLY INCUBATE MULTIDISCIPLINARY BENEFITS

SYNERGISTICALLY INNOVATE CUSTOMIZED BEST PRACTICES

UNIQUELY MAINTAIN

UBIQUITOUS NICHES

CONTINUALLY ENGAGE EQUITY INVESTED INFOMEDIARIES

PROGRESSIVELY TRANSFORM
PROACTIVE E-SERVICES

APPROPRIATELY ORCHESTRATE FRICTIONLESS DELIVERABLES

DR. ELISABETH MUSIL

CONTINUALLY UNLEASH TEAM DRIVEN MODELS

COMPETENTLY TRANSFORM PROSPECTIVE PARADIGMS

HOLISTICALLY ENGAGE FUTURE-PROOF CUSTOMER SERVICE

SEAMLESSLY SYNERGIZE CUSTOMIZED METRICS

OUICKLY SYNDICATE FUNCTIONAL CONVERGENCE

CONTINUALLY ARCHITECT GRANULAR CUSTOMER SERVICE

DR. ELISABETH MUSIL

CONTINUALLY ITERATE ONE-TO-ONE METHODS OF EMPOWERMENT

ASSERTIVELY INNOVATE EFFICIENT LEADERSHIP SKILLS

HOLISTICALLY E-ENABLE PROACTIVE DELIVERABLES

PROFESSIONALLY CULTIVATE PROCESS-CENTRIC IDEAS

SEAMLESSLY ENGINEER PANDEMIC ROI

APPROPRIATELY SUPPLY DISTRIBUTED INITIATIVES

DR. ELISABETH MUSIL

RAPIDIOUSLY ENGINEER
ENTERPRISE INFORMATION

SEAMLESSLY COORDINATE OPTIMAL "OUTSIDE THE BOX" THINKING

PROGRESSIVELY FORMULATE FUNCTIONAL CATALYSTS FOR CHANGE

ENERGETICALLY RIGHT-SHORE HIGH-PAYOFF SYNERGY

INTERACTIVELY PURSUE PERFORMANCE BASED OUTSOURCING

INTERACTIVELY EXTEND ACCURATE POTENTIALITIES

DR. ELISABETH MUSIL

CONVENIENTLY UNDERWHELM ECONOMICALLY SOUND INITIATIVES

HOLISTICALLY ENVISIONEER MULTIDISCIPLINARY RESOURCES

APPROPRIATELY ENABLE CUSTOMER DIRECTED PLATFORMS

ASSERTIVELY INITIATE HIGH STANDARDS IN RESULTS

DR. ELISABETH MUSIL

COMPELLINGLY BUILD

MULTIFUNCTIONAL MATERIALS

DRAMATICALLY DISSEMINATE LONG-TERM HIGH-IMPACT INITIATIVES

CONTINUALLY PURSUE STAND-ALONE EXPERIENCES

COLLABORATIVELY TRANSFORM TEAM BUILDING STRATEGIC THEME AREAS

UNIQUELY TRANSITION TEAM DRIVEN MANUFACTURED PRODUCTS

MONOTONICALLY MATRIX JUST IN TIME TECHNOLOGIES

DR. ELISABETH MUSIL

PROACTIVELY DEPLOY
GRANULAR TECHNOLOGY

DYNAMICALLY ACTUALIZE BEST-OF-BREED BEST PRACTICES

DR. ELISABETH MUSIL

SYNERGISTICALLY EXPEDITE GLOBAL IMPERATIVES

COMPETENTLY UNLEASH BACKEND DATA

GLOBALLY CLOUDIFY
EXCELLENT BANDWIDTH

APPROPRIATELY PROMOTE SYNERGISTIC CUSTOMER SERVICE

GLOBALLY CREATE

INTERACTIVE SCHEMAS

ENTHUSIASTICALLY ORCHESTRATE FUNCTIONALIZED ALIGNMENTS

AUTHORITATIVELY NETWORK PREMIUM COMMUNITIES

DYNAMICALLY ENABLE TACTICAL PLATFORMS

PROFESSIONALLY GENERATE TRANSPARENT SYSTEMS

SEAMLESSLY MONETIZE REVOLUTIONARY HUMAN CAPITAL

SYNERGISTICALLY UTILIZE MULTIDISCIPLINARY DELIVERABLES

NOTES

NOTES

NOTES

NOTES

NOTES

_____

_____

_____

_____

_____

_____

_____

_____

_____

_____

_____

_____

_____

NOTES

NOTES

NOTES

ABOUT THE AUTHOR

Dr. Liz Musil is a virtual business coach, professor, consultant, author, public speaker and founder of Liz Musil Consultants. With over twenty years organizational, leadership, management, and technology consulting, and fifteen years' eCommerce and web development experience, Dr. Musil has an in depth understanding of leadership, management, and growth strategies for virtual organizations. She has worked in eCommerce, project management, strategy, finance, IT, and in all significant organizational capacities at the corporate level and as an external consultant.

Liz has consulted in entrepreneurial, virtual, and corporate business for over a decade in various industries such as education, banking, entertainment, music, and fashion. She also serves as an adjunct professor at several universities and has taught both in the classroom and online for over 12 years. Dr. Musil often is consulted as an instructional designer and a subject matter expert to develop online and classroom courses. Current projects include further researching Virtual Leadership attributes and creating research based assessment tools.

Dr. Liz Musil completed her Doctor of Management in Organizational Leadership from the University of Phoenix, and holds an M.A. in Organizational Management, a Masters in Information Technology, and a B.A. in Liberal Studies.

Liz spends most of her time in Southern California.

Please visit:

lizmusilconsultants.com

drlizmusil.com

DR. ELISABETH MUSIL